THE POWER OF EMOTIONS

Master your emotions in 7 simple steps and take
control of your life

Daniel J. Martin

Note: This book was created with the intention of offering information, suggestions and guidance on different areas of life, including emotional wellbeing, mental health, personal growth and the development of healthy relationships. However, it is in no way a substitute for professional medical attention or counseling from a qualified psychologist or therapist. If you are dealing with serious emotional or mental health issues, we recommend that you seek professional help immediately.

"Life isn't about waiting for the storm to pass. It's about learning to dance in the rain."

— Vivian Greene

CONTENTS

DOWNLOAD THE AUDIOBOOK FREE!

*If you would rather enjoy **The Power of Emotions** while you drive, walk or work out... **Download the audio version totally FREE!***

www.danieljmartin.es/audio/poe

Introduction

Whether you like it or not, we are emotional beings. And whether you accept it or not, how you feel each day affects your quality of life. It's not just me saying this; there is unanimity in the scientific community of human psychology. Emotions are the basis of happiness and personal development. You can have lots of money in the bank and feel unfortunate, or you can have everything in your favor and ruin your life with bad decisions because you don't know how to interpret what you feel.

So, it's better to start a serious dialog with your own emotions. Because feeling them is inevitable, whether you like them or not. What's more, your emotions are there to be listened to, because they're bringing you information and it's your responsibility to learn how to use that information in the same way that you learned how to use your hands.

Of course, some emotions make you feel weak or stupid: sadness, fear, disgust…nobody likes to feel those things. However, I assure you that it's better to feel them than not to: those emotions are being broadcast live from your situation at that moment. Even if your sadness is due to something that happened in the past, it's information about your current situation.

Emotions are pure present. And you already know that you can only act and live in the present. So it's up to you whether you make your emotions your allies, or spend your life battling them. Only you can decide not to turn your back on your emotions in order to obtain a false sense of control over yourself (spoiler alert: you can't get it).

So, what do we do? Do we let ourselves be carried away by emotions? Do we let them dictate what we do at all times, even when it hinders us? No. What you need to do is understand them and educate them. Educating your emotions doesn't mean suppressing them. The former means growing as a person – the latter is impossible.

Emotional expression

Nowadays, there is a lot of importance given to emotional expression in early years education. Even in preschool it's now common to see classroom games that involve manifesting and talking about emotions, so that young children can become familiar with them. And I'm glad. Why? Well, because in my day, only one teacher cared at all what we were feeling as students. What's more, emotions were seen as something destabilizing and problematic, so we were taught to hide them: don't cry, don't get mad, don't yell (even in joy!), don't answer back, don't express yourself. My generation spent the most important years of our personal development repressing and hiding our emotions.

What was this supposed to achieve? Honestly – I have no idea. If they wanted to create "strong" future men and women, they failed completely: many of those boys and girls are now adults suffering from anxiety, depression, sadness or anhedonia [1], not to mention the number of dysfunctional relationships being established.

If someone had taught me when I was little that feeling afraid is a good thing, that crying from sadness is the right thing, that anger is healthy and that all of that formed part of my life... How many falls could I have avoided? How

---

[1] Anhedonia is the total inability to feel pleasure over the nice things in life, whether physical, psychological or social, and it's a clear sign of depression or coercive situations. Its name comes from the opposite of hedonism, which is precisely the opposite: acting exclusively for pleasure.

many feelings of inadequacy, confusion and shame could I have saved myself?

Now that I know it, I want you to know it too: nothing that you feel is bad. No emotion invalidates you as a person, neither professionally nor socially. What you feel is simply information. What you do with that is the part you need to think about.

A pending matter

The book in your hands tackles a pending matter that many of us have carried with us since childhood. It's normal for it to be hard to see the positive side of certain emotions if no one has ever explained to you how important they are. So, this book is for you if:

- Your emotions make you feel ashamed, guilty or inadequate.

- You behave impulsively and often regret your actions.

- You often go from joy to tearfulness.

- You have more painful emotions than satisfying ones.

- You often feel anxious or sad.

- You're stuck in the past.

- You constantly see failure and unfairness in yourself or those around you.

- You "overthink".

If you can relate to what you just read, it's not that something's "not working" with you or that your emotions are crazy: it just means that you're not attending to your own needs.

I ask you to read this book to your own emotions. By the time you finish, you will have got to know yourself in a new way. What way is that? Well, with less fear, less guilt and less shame. You will have understood that your emotions are there to help you.

It's never too late to get to know yourself. It's never too late to let your emotions act as what they are: the material your soul, dreams and happiness are made of.

Read this guide to emotions, and at the end, if you want, let's talk. For now, my only suggestion to you is this: feel however you want!

Daniel J. Martin

What are emotions and what are they for?

"Emotions are the result of how we experience, mentally and physically, our interaction between our internal world and the world outside."

— Elsa Punset

What am I feeling?

To define them academically, we could say that emotions are subjective experiences that appear as a response to certain stimuli. They're natural reactions, automatic and inevitable, that we experience as a result of our perceptions, thoughts, ideas and memories. Their manifestation involves psychophysiological aspects such as accelerated heart rate, smiling, tears or blushing, and mental aspects, such as understanding those reactions on a cognitive level.

Emotions can be intense or subtle, stay for a long time or disappear after a few seconds, and they influence our thoughts and actions just like they influence our mood.

What can an emotion cause?

- **A sensory perception** (interpreted by the brain): hearing an explosion, listening to an upbeat song, feeling someone touch you, looking at a beautiful landscape or watching a movie scene, and so on.

- **A memory:** Past experiences can generate emotions in the present when you remember them.

- **Social interaction of any kind:** A work meeting, a phone conversation or even eye contact can cause anything from tranquility to fear.

- **A belief that contrasts with reality.** For example, if I know that something is unfair and I suffer because of it, I will probably feel emotions that react to that injustice, such as rage, anger or frustration.

- **Biochemical factors:** Emotions are mental products, and the mind works with biochemical material. This means that hormonal changes or organic imbalances that affect your brain chemistry also affect your mood. Low levels of dopamine or serotonin, for example, can cause sadness even with no external factors you can link it to.

Negative emotions

"The idea that you have to be protected from any kind of uncomfortable emotion is what I absolutely do not subscribe to."

— John Cleese

We wrongly consider that some of our emotions are negative and others positive. We understand negative emotions to be those we perceive as destabilizing, dangerous or unpleasant, while positive ones are those that bring us satisfaction and calm. However, we shouldn't judge them this way: emotions in themselves are neither good nor bad, nor should we feel guilty about feeling them. As David Kessler [2] explains, what we should be concerned with is what we do with them:

"You are not responsible for your feelings, but you are responsible for what you do with them."

The emotions of your life

Human beings generate and feel dozens of emotions every day. We can also provoke emotions in others, whether we're aware we're doing it or not.

---

[2] David Kessler is a psychology expert famous for his contributions in the field of emotional management linked to grief.

All these emotions are like waves: they are created, they come, they go and they disappear, one after the other. Most of them barely last a few minutes. If the seas are calm, they are pleasant and we can receive them without problems. If the seas are choppy, they pound against us and can even be dangerous.

Humans are capable of feeling over a hundred different emotions, although not all with the same frequency. Below, I've put together a list of some that most of us feel, to a greater or lesser extent[3]:

1. Joy
2. Sadness
3. Fear
4. Rage
5. Surprise
6. Disgust
7. Love
8. Hatred
9. Guilt
10. Tenderness

---

[3] Only individuals with personality disorders such as psychopathy or narcissism are left out of most of these emotions.

You might be wondering: "So, where's anxiety? Isn't that an emotion, too?".

It's true that many psychologists consider it one more emotion, but I think it's more fitting to say that anxiety is a defense mechanism that uses emotions. It is triggered in the brain in order to get your attention, and that's why all the emotions linked to anxiety are intense and unpleasant. In addition, the more you try to ignore that anxiety, the more the brain charges it with sharp and frequent emotions until we fulfil our duty to listen to it.

Similar to anxiety, there are other states that are not technically emotions, but that do bring with them subjective experiences linked to the emotional system, such as:

- apathy or boredom

- weariness

- hope

- infatuation

- inner peace or wellbeing

- motivation

- grief

All of these are states of mind that vary depending on your circumstances, and they involve a similar set of emotions in each case.

What are emotions for?

Emotions are information and their function is adaptable. In the same way that you feel cold, itchy or headachy because your brain manifests it in order to make you act accordingly (put a sweater on, scratch or take a painkiller), you may perceive that you are scared, angry or happy about something.

These are their main functions:

- **Personalization of the information around you:** The information around you and that comes via your senses needs to be "personalized" in order to be useful. So, emotions accompany every stimulus and give it "extra" meaning. For example, when it rains, your brain may conclude that this is positive because there has been a drought, or negative if you don't want to get wet. It then generates an emotion that expresses that to help you understand how the rain is going to affect you.

- **Adaptation:** Usually, emotions are also indicating what your response should be to external demands. If you perceive a threat, you feel fear in order to indicate to you that you need to react immediately through fight or flight.

- **Communication:** Emotions are a form of non-verbal communication. Via expressions such as smiling, spontaneous tone of voice, hand gestures, body posture, physiological reactions like blushing, and so on, emotions help to appropriately send the message you want to transmit to those around you, even if you don't realize it or want them to. In this sense, emotional communication doesn't always work in your favor; it simply responds to what your brain decides it needs to do to protect your survival, regardless of whether it's "socially acceptable" or "gives you away".

- **Mental logging and decision-making:** Emotions affect the way you assess each situation, in the thoughts or lessons you take from it or the way you store it as a memory. As memories are linked to emotions, they can lead you to make one decision or another accordingly. For example, emotions linked to past traumas condition your behavior in the present.

An example: What is anger for?

Now, let's imagine a situation you perceive to be unfair, such as somebody deliberately disrespecting you. The most natural emotion linked to this situation would be anger: a very intense sensation that brings with it feelings of frustration, danger, rage and so on. What purpose does that anger serve?

1. **Detecting the violation of personal boundaries:** Anger goes off like a car alarm in order to manifest that the person in question is crossing a line and that your physical or psychological integrity is under attack.

2. **Self-affirmation:** In an unfair or abusive situation, anger is your brain's way of reminding you that you have a right to personal wellbeing and respect.

3. **Mobilizing change:** Anger serves as a driver for motivation and action in order to stop that situation.

Bearing this in mind, do you really think that anger is negative and that it's better not to feel it? I don't think so: in an unfair or abusive situation, you should welcome anger!

So, when you're experiencing anger, you have three choices. Decide for yourself which is most aligned with your interests:

- **Option 1**: Be overcome with anger and consider it a problem that's adding to the initial problem, meaning you now have two problems.

- **Option 2**: Act impulsively in following that emotion, so you may stop the situation, but you generate even worse consequences.

- **Option 3:** Understand what is causing you to feel angry, without getting carried away by primary impulses.

In a family dynamic where one member is always disrespecting you, the anger you feel indicates that you cannot allow it to carry on. What should you do? It may be that the change comes when you slam your fist down on the table or start yelling, but it's more likely to be smarter not to lose control and to get ready to close the door on that family member and anyone who takes his or her side.

In this case, anger, however visceral and overwhelming it feels, is not asking you to act unthinkingly or reactively, but to recognize that change on your part is now necessary. The harder you try "not to think about it" or "let it go", the stronger your inner anger will get.

Summary of Chapter 1

–   Emotions are subjective, automatic and inevitable reactions to perceived stimuli.

–   Emotions are simply information for the driver and they serve two purposes: informative (on how your surroundings are affecting you) and adaptive (how you should act as a consequence).

–   Humans can feel over a hundred different emotions.

–   Emotions are neither positive nor negative; it's what you do with them that leads to a good or bad action.

–   Sometimes, what we're afraid of about an emotion (like anger) is not the emotion itself but what it causes us to do. We often believe that anger causes us to be violent or visceral, when it's actually leading us to inevitable change.

How your emotional system works

"Emotions are not interruptions to thought; they are an integral part of it."

— Antonio Damasio

Your nervous system is in charge of producing your responses to external stimuli, and its nucleus is the brain. The brain is the most sophisticated organ and it is made up of billions of nerve cells (neurons), which communicate with each other through electrical impulses and chemical reactions, forming a complex network of connection.

Neuroscience has long been able to identify in this extraordinary system the areas of the brain that influence the creation of emotional experiences. We know that the amygdala, a little "almond"[4] located in the middle of the brain, is key to the management of fear and our fight-or-flight response to it – and also, that it is responsible for detecting situations with emotional baggage. The prefrontal cortex is related to emotional regulation and decision-making based on feelings.

Neuroscience has also revealed the extent to which emotions are pure chemistry: substances such as serotonin, dopamine and noradrenaline are neurotransmitters (like the gas in your car) that play a crucial role in expressing emotions. That's why a hormonal imbalance can induce a certain mood regardless of external circumstances.

---

[4] In fact, the word "amygdala" comes from the Greek for "almond".

The thoughts-actions-emotions triangle

The emotional responses your nervous system produces do not work in isolation: they are interwoven with other mental dynamics in such a way that they affect your beliefs and thoughts and, in turn, lead you to carry out certain actions. In the same way, these actions and thoughts condition certain emotions. These three elements form a triangle with three vertices that are constantly feeding into each other:

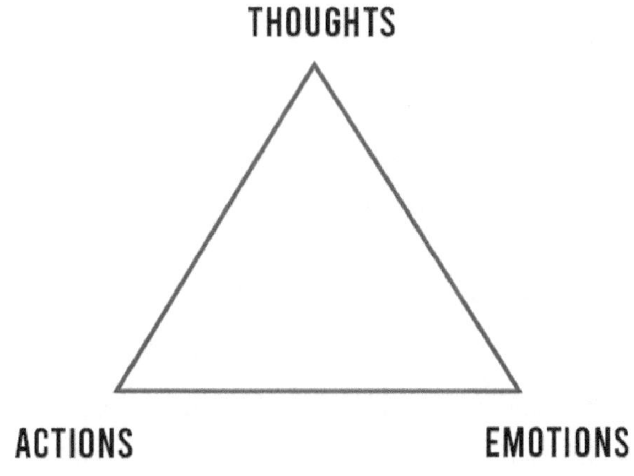

- **Thoughts:** The cognitive processes that happen with all the information you receive from outside. These cognitive processes result in learning, memory, ideas, working memory, habits, judgments and prejudices, beliefs, and so on.

- **Emotions:** We've already talked about these being the subjective responses you experience in relation to stimuli and your interpretation of them: sadness, happiness, anger, surprise, disgust, joy, love, and so on. The stimuli you perceive through your senses can provoke a wide range of emotions depending on how they are considered or interpreted by the brain. Remember the rain example: emotions help you to understand what the rain means for you in terms of benefits or disadvantages.

- **Actions:** Your active behaviors, or in other words, the things you do consciously and voluntarily in response to your emotions and thoughts. Actions are not just physical acts, but also the verbal communication you produce consciously.

Now, let's imagine you hold a deep-seated belief about the dangers of public speaking (stage fright). Although you know on a rational level that there is no actual risk to your survival (nobody ever died of stage fright), your primitive brain[5] thinks that public speaking is a risky act, so every time you have to do it, it triggers a series of uncomfortable and unpleasant emotions to make you avoid public speaking and therefore "keep you safe".

Let's say, despite that, you gradually face your fear of public speaking, expose yourself to doing it and one day even do it really well. Throughout that process, your emotions will have changed: through your actions, you will have created

---

[5] We give the name "primitive brain" to the part of our minds that are only looking out for our safety and survival, without caring about social conventions or circumstances that have nothing to do with keeping us alive.

"proof" that you can speak in public with no risk to your survival, and your deeply-held belief that it's impossible for you to do will begin to disappear. In this case, thoughts, actions and emotions have followed a joint process in order to get rid of a phenomenon that they themselves created a long time ago when they gave you stage fright in the first place.

Distorted thinking and irrational beliefs can lead you to feel emotions that are totally real but which are responding to a danger that is not real. These emotions feed into the thought, and all of this takes you further away from the action which will benefit you in the long term. This is true, for example, of panic attacks or anxiety crises. If you can understand that all of it forms part of a circuit where beliefs and reality are often not the same as each other, you can begin to better understand the messages sent by your nervous system. If you can control your responses to those messages, you can control your actions and beliefs, and that makes your emotions change.

Neural discomfort

Let's take a look at another example of how that triangle of thoughts, emotions and actions works. This one is based on what's known as "neural discomfort" and it's highly illustrative of how your emotions can feed into erroneous thoughts and unsuitable actions, and vice versa. To begin with, do you know what neural discomfort is?

Neural discomfort is the mental resistance to carrying out a task that you don't like or that you perceive as annoying, useless or unpleasant. It could be an unexpected guest who turns up right when you're about to go out in a hurry and makes the situation worse.

That neural discomfort manifests as emotions that suggest not doing something, and it's common for it to "visit" any time you have a task that puts you in a bad mood or that you don't feel like doing: needing to make an important decision, take a difficult phone call, and so on.

Why does neural discomfort arise? We've already talked about how your primitive brain, when it's trying to protect you, doesn't hesitate to send you uncomfortable emotions in order to get you to react. The same thing happens when you think you're going to be "wasting time and energy" on something you perceive to be pointless. All of this is good news; it means your self-preservation system is working. The bad news is that you need to figure out when your brain is tricking you.

What can you do about neural discomfort? Experiments surrounding this have shown that, if you accept that discomfort without giving into it – in other words, if you tackle the "problematic" task even when you feel uncomfortable – all those unpleasant emotions (bad mood, anger, frustration, anxiety and so on) tend to disappear. And, since your brain has an emotional memory too, your neural discomfort toward those situations will gradually decrease over time.

By doing this, you can manage to:

- Accept and understand your emotions with regard to x unpleasant task.

- Stop acting against your own interests (not doing the tasks you know you need to do), and learn to act even with a cacophony of emotions urging you not to.

- Change your future emotions and thoughts linked to that task, so it will get easier and easier to do it.

You have modified the "natural" course of the triangle. That shows that the thoughts-emotions-actions triangle can be consciously changed. That said, don't expect the neural discomfort to disappear overnight if you have always experienced it when facing certain tasks. And that applies to any situation that makes you feel worn out, nervous, bored: going to the gym, cleaning the house, studying for a test, resolving an issue that's been bugging you, making that awkward phone call, going to the dentist, taking a cold shower, following the diet your doctor recommended, and so on. Only when you have repeated that action or habit several times with an attitude of acceptance toward your own reluctance can your brain stop sabotaging you.

One way of guiding and training your own emotions to stop sabotaging you at the worst possible times is to practice uncomfortable activities. This isn't about punishing yourself; it's about training yourself.

Summary of Chapter 2

–   Your nervous system is in charge of receiving information, interpreting it and producing responses accordingly.

–   This process of managing information gives rise to a closed circuit in the form of a triangle between your thoughts, emotions and actions.

–   If you can control that triangle, you will live the way you want and deserve, no matter what.

–   Every time you continue to carry out a task despite neural discomfort, you show your brain the benefits of doing so. Your brain then understands that the benefits outweigh the potential problems, so you'll find it increasingly easier to do.

Accepting you are an emotional being

"Don't be afraid of your fears. They're not there to scare you. They're there to let you know that something is worth it."

— Joy Bell

The first thing you need to understand in order to learn to manage your emotions is that you cannot reject them. All your emotions are valid, however unpleasant they are or however much they hurt you when they arise.

Emotions are part of the human condition itself, which means you can't *not* feel them, just like you can't never smile or feel hungry or thirsty. If they're part of our existence, why do we reject them?

I already pointed to it in the introduction: one way or another, we're taught to when we're children, to stop them "getting out of hand" or "knocking us off balance". Although, as long as we're alive, that balance can't be broken: with every new life stage, every new experience, every sickness, problem, failure or success, we get knocked off balance – not to mention falling in love, being bereaved or being betrayed by someone.

So it's okay to be overcome by emotion from time to time. It's okay to feel angry, jealous, powerless, sad, guilty or embarrassed. And it's okay to feel so much joy that you want to jump around screaming, too.

If your emotions leave you confused, ashamed or uncomfortable, ask yourself:

- Why do I think that feeling this way is wrong or shameful?

- How am I supposed to feel instead?

- What would have stopped me from feeling this discomfort?

In many cases, discomfort over your own emotions comes from past experiences: getting yelled at in school, being told your behavior was inappropriate when you were learning to manage your feelings, discovering that emotions can "trick" you (it's actually the beliefs associated with them that do that), and of course distrusting your own feelings...

In particular, I often come across men who have trouble accepting their emotional sides. It makes them feel weak, vulnerable or stupid. "Men shouldn't get scared," they tell themselves. In fact, the opposite is true. It's often our emotional systems that keep us alive and integrated in society.

Being "too emotional"

In my line of work, I often see men who complain that their partners or other women in their lives are "unstable", intense or hard to relate to in terms of feelings. In the same way, I hear a lot of women saying they're embarrassed of "feeling too much" or being "emotional rollercoasters". I understand the discomfort and disadvantages that can generate, but in no way is that the fault of the women themselves.

Many emotional disagreements between men and women come from the differences between our limbic systems[6], which are linked to the manifestation of emotions. Add to that the effect of sex hormones in many of the life stages of women which don't correspond to those of men: menstrual cycles, pregnancy and post-partum, to name the best-known examples, carry with them adjustments that are *natural* (that is, normal and inevitable from a physiological point of view),

---

[6] I'm not trying to limit reality to the man-woman binary, I'm just discussing what I encounter in my profession when tackling problems in heterosexual relationships.

and which translate into the "mood swings" that women are the predominant victims of.

Add to that cultural and historic factors. We still live in patriarchal societies where men can focus on their careers while women are supposed to meet high expectations in many fields at once: work, family, motherhood, housework, social conventions, beauty standards, caring for older relatives, and so on.

As if all of that weren't enough to create differences in opinion, even in contexts of full equality, men and women feel things differently. Most studies have found that, on average, women tend to have more empathy than men. This means that they are more sensitive to others' emotions and, naturally, they are more predisposed to solidarity and to "carrying" the emotions generated by others' suffering or problems[7].

All of this means that women are often considered "more emotional" than men. But that doesn't mean men are superior because they "feel less" or are less empathetic. In fact, anthropology tells us that what helped us to evolve as a species was specifically our predisposition to cooperate and act in solidarity based on empathy.

When did we begin to consider men's way of feeling things "right" and women's "wrong"? I don't know, but while ever it's still considered that way, upset and disagreements are guaranteed to keep happening.

"Feminine" vs. "masculine" emotions

---

[7] I'm speaking generally here. I'm sure you know a woman with no emotional problems who might even use her gender to take advantage of men. They do exist, but believe me: for every woman doing this, there are twenty men doing it the other way around.

If you're not clear about this, let me give you an example of how emotions are accepted in typically masculine contexts, in comparison with how they are rejected in feminine contexts.

In many countries, male emotions associated with sporting events are normalized. It would be rare for a man to be embarrassed of "feeling too much" when his soccer team is playing an important final. It's accepted that those men get emotional, yell, get frustrated, and so on. However, a woman crying or being sad about some misfortune going on thousands of miles away is seen as a sign of weakness or immaturity: her feelings are looked down upon because "that's just how the world works" or "it happens every day, you can't cry about it". Why is it immature to feel empathy with someone else's suffering, but it's not immature to roar with excitement when a guy who doesn't know you from Adam puts a ball into a net? It makes no sense.

*"True happiness comes from living genuinely and
letting your emotions flow without judgment."*

— Carl Rogers

The conclusion is that men and women feel things in different ways. Invalidating, ignoring or judging the emotions of the opposite sex is not just unfair, it's also totally pointless. Instead, let's try to empathize more with how those around us feel.

Your cookies are for people who appreciate them

This is another subject entirely. I'm a firm believer in not hiding your emotions. However, not every moment is optimal and not every person is suitable for sharing your emotions with. Let me explain with an analogy.

Imagine you baked some fabulous chocolate chip cookies. To cool them faster, you leave them on a tray on the windowsill (like they used to do in villages). Since your window is at street level, people walking by can smell the cookies. Attracted by the aroma, several people come over to the tray. What are their intentions? Well, some people will want to compare your cookies with the ones they bake at home. Others are just looking for a way to steal them. Others will be so impressed that they'll want to meet the creator, maybe chat to you about baking tips. And someone will fall in love with your cookies and suggest getting them together with their croissants.

Well, those cookies are your emotions. And emotions, like the smell of fresh cookies, attract people. It's instinctive. But, as you can see, not everyone has good intentions when walking up to other people's cookies. So be careful and don't wear your heart on your sleeve for everyone you meet.

That said, would it be safer never to show your feelings at all? In truth, no: firstly, because we've already said that that's impossible, and secondly, because it's dehumanizing.

Not feeling things or not showing your feelings is not the answer: the wonderful people who are going to love you, the people who appreciate you, hope to share your more emotional side with you. In fact, it's impossible to love someone if you can't access their emotions. All you have to do is not give them out to just anyone without knowing if they're going to use them carefully.

Accepting yourself here and now

Accepting yourself means acknowledging that you are vulnerable and imperfect, while still being worthy of love, regardless of what others think or of the mistakes you may have made.

Accepting your emotional side is the first step to achieving wellbeing, and it involves accepting the emotions brought on by your physical state, your past, your mistakes and your limitations.

Accepting all these things, like I always say, doesn't mean being happy about them, or agreeing with them, or being passionate about living life under those circumstances – it means that that's the way things are. If someone is terrified of air travel, they have to accept that, right at that moment, that's how it is. If someone is ashamed to get naked in front of somebody, they need to accept that there are a few things about their body that they feel uncomfortable with. The emotions that brings just mean that their beliefs about how reality should be and the way reality actually is are misaligned.

The more things you can accept about yourself and about your surroundings (again: "accept" doesn't mean love), the fewer negative reactions you will suffer, the less energy you will expend on enduring the "shame" of feeling that way, and the more predisposed to change you'll be.

Do you know how you usually feel?

Do you know what your most frequent emotions are? Would you be able to say how intensely you feel sadness, bitterness or hope?

I invite you to write a list of the emotions you know, or use the list from chapter one. Over the next week, check off every emotion that you feel, every time you feel it. If you can, add a brief note about when you felt it, what you were doing at that time and why you think you felt that emotion and not a different one. If you felt ashamed of that emotion, reflect on why and on what could have happened to stop you feeling that way.

Over time, you'll learn to accept all emotions equally and you'll realize that the emotions you considered negative have come to seem less threatening or absurd. As you reflect on them and see when they tend to arise, you'll find them all much more logical and much more helpful – and you will no longer view yourself as an uncontrollably emotional being.

Summary of Chapter 3

–   All your emotions are valid.

–   Traditional education teaches you to hide your emotions, so most of us are not trained to manage them.

–   Generally speaking, men and women feel things differently. Invalidating the emotions of the opposite sex is not just unfair – it's inaccurate.

–   Not everyone deserves for you to share your emotions with them: your emotions are for people who can appreciate them.

How to work on your emotions

"It's not about eliminating negative emotions, but about reducing their intensity."

— Jonathan García-Allen

We've already looked at how feeling emotions is part of the human condition, and that their function is adaptive. We've also seen how they form part of a system that can become contaminated if we don't regulate it. In this chapter, we will look at how and why we should regulate our emotions. To begin with, we're going to talk about emotional intelligence.

What is emotional intelligence?

Emotional intelligence is the ability to understand and regulate emotions in order to avoid being enslaved by them or led into inaccurate beliefs. Emotional intelligence is linked to not ignoring calls to action and not evading responsibilities. In the words of Daniel Goleman[8]:

"Emotional intelligence is not just knowing your emotions, but being able to manage them."

It was the psychologist Wayne Payne who coined the expression "emotional intelligence"[9] to refer to this ability to tend to your own emotions properly, although other researchers had already indicated the importance of including a person's emotional side when assessing their skills.

Emotional intelligence is the capacity to recognize your own emotions and those of others,

---

[8] Daniel Goleman is an American psychologist who shot to fame with his 1995 book *Emotional Intelligence.*

[9] He did so in his doctoral thesis *A Study of Emotion: Developing Emotional Intelligence* (1985), considered pioneering in this field of research.

differentiate between them, use them as information for knowing, learning and thinking, and adapting all those emotions to each environment or situation. Let's say, if baking is based on the correct management of ingredients in order to create cakes, emotional intelligence is based on the correct management of emotions to obtain the right results in terms of physical, mental and social health.

Managing your emotions doesn't mean repressing or distorting them. It means making the most of their potential. In the same way that a baker maneuvers ingredients to get the most out of them in order to make cakes, emotional intelligence maneuvers emotions.

Why is it so important to be able to regulate your emotions? There are lots of reasons, but here is one as important as it is neglected: whatever you don't control, you leave open to other people controlling. And if other people control it, believe me: you'll never be the one who benefits most.

Correctly expressing your emotions

In many cases, the emotional burden we carry comes from not expressing our emotional needs properly to those around us, or from not knowing how to respond correctly to the emotions of others. It's your responsibility to be able to communicate, so you have to learn how to do it. If you feel that this is hard for you, it would be helpful to follow these steps:

1. When you're going to communicate something that's emotionally loaded, you first need to know what emotions it has generated for you. For example, what emotions does it generate when your partner breaks a promise they made you?

2. Before tackling this conversation, you need to know what you want the other person to

understand. Do you want to tell them that you're hurt and that you expect them to make it up to you? Or that the broken trust is irreparable and that you've decided not to continue with the relationship? What would you like that person to do now?

3. When it comes to expressing yourself, you should use a tone of voice that is firm but not aggressive, get straight to the point and don't explain more than you need to. You should also find the right moment to do this.

4. Start with "I" language, not "you" or accusations: "I feel really hurt and surprised that you didn't keep your promise." You don't need to yell or hurl insults to show that you're hurt: if that person cares about you, they will listen. If they don't, they won't listen, or worse: they will manipulate you or go on the defensive.

5. Don't bring up other topics or attack the other person's character. Don't manipulate them into feeling guilty, either, or try to convince

them you're "right". Just communicate and wait for their response. Something like: "I'd like to know why you didn't keep your promise and how we can be more responsible with our commitments in the future."

Communicating your emotions in this way is based on being assertive, which is the ability and the right to manifest your thoughts, emotions and needs without being invalidated by it.

When you communicate assertively, you are not inciting conflict. From there, the other person should listen and respond without invalidating you: if they do, you need to think carefully about the possibility that that person doesn't care about your feelings.

Here are some examples of how I and some of my clients have decided to express emotions:

-   I don't agree with how you treat me. I feel frustrated by it. I wish we could have more respectful communication. I hope you understand.

- I feel sad you didn't answer my calls. I know you don't have a lot of time, but I feel that I'm not a priority for you. If that's the case, I'm asking you to tell me so.

- I'm worried about the project we need to finish. I'm afraid we won't get it done on time. Can we discuss some options and assign tasks more clearly?

- I'm really happy about my achievement. I want to share my joy with you and thank you for your support throughout the process. How can I show you how grateful I am?

Actively listening

In the same way that you need to learn to speak more responsible in terms of emotions, you need to learn to listen. This happens when you display a respectful attitude, cooperate (even when you don't agree), express that you've understood the person's point of view (if that's the case), and get ready to find a solution that doesn't involve telling the other person what they "have" to do or getting mad. In short:

- Listen to what the other person is saying instead of planning what to say while they talk.

- Don't interrupt.

- Don't look for ways to show them they're wrong (tell them they're right when they are).

- Don't get defensive: there's no need to if the person is not attacking you. If they do attack you or they become disrespectful, remove yourself.

- Practice empathy and try to understand how the other person might be feeling.

- Ask open-ended questions and show genuine interest in finding a solution.

- Don't invalidate their emotions.

Active listening doesn't mean you can't disagree. It means accepting responsibility in conflict and respecting others' emotions.

How to say "no"

We've already mentioned that active listening and a respectful attitude don't mean agreeing with the other person. Sometimes, you have to reject suggestions, requests or solutions to conflict that you don't agree with. How can you say "no" when there is emotional baggage?

1. Before speaking, make sure you understand the request and what it involves. If you don't understand something, don't be afraid to ask. If the request is dishonest, abusive or unfair, don't get offended: a firm "no" is always better than a long argument about how inappropriate the request is.

2. Before saying no, do a mental exercise: why are you saying no? Is it a real no or is there

any bitterness or defiance in it for you? Would your "no" change if some of the conditions of the request were different?

3. Once you're clear on the reasons for your "no", assess which of them you can share with the other person. Being honest doesn't always involve giving excessive explanations.

4. Bearing that in mind, don't be afraid to give your answer. "I've been thinking about your proposal, but I've decided not to accept for x reason," or "I understand what you're saying, but I don't think that's for me/it's not going to work for me right now/I don't like it/I'm not ready." When you do this, remember that you're not trying to convince the other person of your reasons. Your only aim is to communicate your "no". The other person's reaction is not your responsibility.

5. If appropriate, offer alternatives or negotiate. If you open space for negotiation, make it clear that your answer to the initial suggestion is still "no". The negotiation is about other

options, not a manipulation with blackmail until you accept the original suggestion.

6. If they don't accept, stand firm in your "no". For example: "As I said, I've already decided on this point, and I can't help you/I'm not the person you're looking for/I really don't feel like it/I've made it clear I don't want to do that." If they insist: "It's bothering me that you keep insisting on this. I feel like you want to persuade me without respecting my point of view or my freedom of choice. I'm asking you to respect my 'no'."

7. Don't accuse the other person of trying to manipulate or coerce you, even if they are. Why? Because if you do, they will deny it and accuse you and the discussion will turn into you having to justify your words instead of focusing on saying "no". Don't focus on what they're saying: ignore any threats (only while you're speaking to them, you can reflect on that later) and calmly continue saying no.

8. When you consider that your position has been clearly expressed, get ready to remove yourself from the conversation and not come back to it.

If the disagreement turns into a fight...

What if the other person doesn't react the way you hoped? What if you can't agree?

You must accept that you can't control the actions, thoughts or feelings of others, but you can (and should!) choose how you act and respond. In cases where there is no room for agreement, the correct management of the situation involves:

- Staying calm: Don't get carried away by provocation or a lack of respect. Focus on your wellbeing and your goal. One trick is to speak quietly and slowly, even if the other person starts yelling.

- Don't change your mind or give in in order to "keep the peace". If you thought something was unfair at the beginning of the discussion, stick with that.

- Mentally remind yourself of your right to be respected: your feelings are valid and legitimate, regardless of what people say.

- Declare your boundaries and consequences. For example: "I won't tolerate this treatment. If you continue to disrespect me, I'll know you're choosing to do it and that you're not interested in resolving this."

- If the other person shows no signs of wanting to resolve the conflict, removing yourself from the situation is usually the best course of action.

- Seek support or proof: If the disrespect or invalidation is constant in a relationship, it's a good idea to find someone you trust or a mental health professional so you can get their perspective and support. If the lack of respect involves denying the evidence, you could always gather some proof.

- Weigh up your options: depending on the seriousness of the situation, you should consider ways to get out. Remember, when weighing up your options, you should never go against your dignity or moral integrity.

Why am I insisting so hard on these points? Because a lot of people's emotional malaise comes from situations where they act against their integrity or dignity, for example to keep the peace or to win someone's approval. That's when your primitive brain rebels and sends you discomfort to make you react.

Your emotional rights

There are many social situations that can make you feel a profound sense of injustice. And while your physical integrity is recognized by law in most countries, your psychological rights are more of a gray area or are simply not acknowledged.

That's why it's important to know your rights when it comes to defending your emotional integrity. In this sense, there are 17 assertive rights that have been recognized for years, coined by Dr Olga Castanyer[10]. They are as follows:

1. The right to be treated with respect and dignity.

2. The right to hold and express your own feelings and opinions.

3. The right to be heard and taken seriously.

4. The right to judge your needs, establish your priorities and make your own decisions.

5. The right to say "NO" without guilt.

---

[10] Olga Castanyer is a psychologist who specializes in self-esteem, emotional rights and assertiveness. Among other books, she wrote the bestseller *Assertiveness: An expression of healthy self-esteem.*

6. The right to ask for what you want, bearing in mind that the other person also has the right to say "no".

7. The right to change.

8. The right to make mistakes.

9. The right to ask for information and to be informed.

10. The right to obtain something you have paid for.

11. The right to decide not to be assertive (without disrespecting others).

12. The right to independence.

13. The right to decide what to do with your property, body, time and so on, as long as it doesn't violate the rights of others.

14. The right to be successful.

15. The right to enjoyment.

16. The right to rest and solitude.

17. The right to better yourself, even if it means overtaking others.

Knowing these rights doesn't mean they'll always be respected (sadly, they tend to get trampled all over) – it means knowing that the logical and natural reaction of your nervous system when these rights are not respected is that of emotional malaise.

Hijacking the brain

A sustained lack of emotional regulation can lead to a loss of free will. Whether because emotions are being repressed in the hope of some "reward" or because you "can't deal with them", a lack of emotional management can hijack your brain. You stop being free and stop acting in accordance with your best interests. This tends to result in dynamics such as:

- Anxiety (and panic attacks and GAD[11]).

- Depression.

- Stress and Post-Traumatic Stress Disorder (PTSD).

- Eating disorders (ED).

- Sleep disorders.

- Somatic symptom disorders (SSD) or somatization.

- Hypochondria.

- Phobias (agoraphobia, fear of flying, etc.).

- Addictions.

- Impulse control disorders (from compulsive buying to pathological lying).

When emotions lose their protective and adaptative function or begin to foster self-destruction, you need to take action. In most cases, professional intervention is necessary and

---

[11] Generalized Anxiety Disorder.

there are very specific treatments for rebalancing the emotional load.

Emotional management therapy

There are dozens of types of treatment and approaches to working on emotions, meaning that we are increasingly aware of their importance. Below, I will list some of the most widely used in the field of clinical psychology:

<u>Emotional regulation therapy:</u>

This is a therapeutic approach that holds emotions up as the key to healing our minds. This therapy focuses on learning to identify and regulate intensely dysfunctional emotions. Their aim is to help you understand why these emotions arise, stop being afraid of them and modulate them in order to stop them from incapacitating you. How is this achieved?

- Understanding your own emotions and their how and why.

- Losing your fear of stressful emotions.

- Working on your self-esteem and confidence.

- Learning about conflict resolution, both with yourself and with others.

- Finding ways to redirect emotions linked to the past.

- Improving communication and social skills.

- Managing manifestations of anger, rage, frustration, sadness and so on.

Exposure therapy:

Exposure therapy is a treatment based on the emotion of fear, used for anxiety disorders, phobias and panic attacks. This treatment claims that exposing yourself to the source of your phobias in a controlled way can help you get over your fear of them.

With exposure therapy, a series of situations relating to the object of fear or anxiety are developed, where the situations become more and more threatening. For example, if you have a fear of flying, the first step could be looking at photos of airports. As your anxiety in response to those photos decreases, you go up a step on the fear hierarchy until you reach simulations and visualizations. In this case, the objective is for the person to be able to travel by plane without suffering panic attacks.

The process of exposure is accompanied by breathing and relaxation techniques, distraction strategies, cognitive restructuring of the threatening beliefs, and more.

Emotionally focused therapy:

Emotionally focused therapy (or EFT) is based on the idea that conflict in relationships arises because of unmet emotional needs. It was developed by Dr Sue Johnson[12] in the 2000s and is aimed at relationships either between partners or in families.

With EFT, the underlying emotions are identified along with their root causes. Bonds and empathy toward the emotions of the other person are also worked on, and it aims to reach an agreement that involves compromise by both parties. All of this is done by fostering:

- Trust in the other person.

- Respect for their independence and freedom.

- The creation of secure bonds.

- Adequate communication.

- The resolution of deep-seated conflict.

____

[12] Sue Johnson is the founding director of the International Centre for Excellence in Emotionally Focused Therapy and author of the bestseller Hold Me Tight.

- Not project or transmitting past relationships to the current one.

There are other approaches (in fact, most psychological therapies work on emotions), such as cognitive behavioral therapy (CBT), solution-focused (SF) therapy, systemic family therapy, and more. Over the next few chapters, we will look at behavioral activation (BA) therapy and acceptance and compromise therapy (ACT), which is a third-generation approach, among others.

Summary of Chapter 4

—   Emotional intelligence is the ability to detect, understand and guide emotions.

—   A lack of skill when it comes to communicating or defending your interests is a significant source of emotional malaise.

—   There is a series of emotional rights that we should all know about, such as the right to be treated with respect, the right to say "no", the right to pursue happiness, etc.

—   Brain hijacking occurs when emotions stop you from being free. This is when disorders arise (anxiety, impulse control issues, eating disorders, etc.), phobias and addictions.

—   There are many treatments aimed at rebalancing emotions.

Educate the way you think

"Our quality of thinking determines our quality of life."
— Brian Tracy

There is a golden rule in the field of emotional management: if you inform the way you think, you'll change the way you feel.

Over sixty thousand thoughts run through your mind every day; most of them are recurrent and automatic, so they go unnoticed. And, even if you don't realize it, those thoughts provoke emotions.

Sixty thousand thoughts a day! How can you inform those sixty thousand daily thoughts, if you're not even aware of most of them?

Well, because it's not about the content of each of those thoughts, but about the dynamic that generated them. Only when you're aware of the type of thinking you're generating can you begin to think differently, and only then can you change your emotions so that they function effectively.

The problem – other than the sheer number of thoughts we all have – is that our "thought generator machine" is subject to many factors and experiences accumulated over decades. Our mindset is the fruit of our education, environment, past traumas and current life situation. Among our thoughts we find a mix of memories with their consequent emotional load, false beliefs, distorted ideas, lessons learned, biases and so on.

Fortunately, it's possible to give your thoughts a good clean the same way you'd clean out your closet or basement. In this chapter, we will look at some strategies for this "mental tidy-up".

Strategy 1: Detecting useless recurring thoughts

Many negative thoughts are a total waste of energy. This first strategy involves turning yourself into a traffic warden for your own thoughts, detecting those that bring nothing: those that serve no adaptative purpose.

Every time you spot a negative thought "driving" around, you need to stop it and ask to see its "license". In the event that that thought has a good reason to be driving, you can let it continue. If not – if all it's doing is jamming up the road and causing emotional discomfort for no good reason – give it a "ticket". You can write that ticket out in your notebook or diary, alongside why you think you have it, for example.

To make this easier, you should know that all automatic, distorted, twisted or non-adaptative thoughts tend to fall into one of the following groups:

- Constantly criticizing and punishing yourself for every mistake.

- Worrying about things in the past you can't change.

- Frequent fear over the future in terms of "fortune telling", in other words "knowing" what's going to happen.

- Catastrophic thinking.

- Recurrent bitterness that's not accompanied by a search for emotional reparations.

- Stewing on injustices that are out of your control.

- Constantly comparing yourself to others.

- Dichotomic, or black-and-white, thinking: either total success or failure, valid or useless, with you or against you, and so on.

- Pushing away the positives so you don't "let your guard down".

- Constant competitive thinking.

- Victim mentality that only serves to confirm you are a victim, not to seek change.

- Constant lack of trust in those around you.

- Self-sabotage.

- Arrogance, haughtiness or condescending thoughts, like "I'm the only one who does any work around here".

- Ritual thoughts leading to extremely rigid habits.

- Limiting thoughts based on tradition, religion, a warped sense of duty and similar.

We all have thoughts like these. But if you're aware of them and can give them a "ticket", you'll soon find that those thoughts stop occupying so much space on your mental road, and more useful cognitive processes and ideas can flourish. All of this will make your state of mind change from one of pessimism, conformism or constant suffering to one of greater wellbeing.

Strategy 2: Imagine the worst

Your thoughts are your perception of reality, but that perception is often distorted and carries hidden emotions that aim to "warn" you of catastrophes and imminent misfortunes that, in actual fact, are neither that bad nor that likely.

When it comes to this, it's a good idea to deliberately attend to each of those thoughts, instead of trying to swat them away like flies. What you need to do is voluntarily think the worst.

Ask yourself: "What is the worst thing that can happen in this situation?". Get right to the heart of the matter, mentally relish the most terrible consequences, no matter how unlikely, of your current decision or situation ending in real disaster. Mentally or physically note down every painful detail of that hypothetical awfulness. Don't look for silver linings, just go right down to the depths of the darkest hole.

Then, ask yourself: "In that extreme situation, is there a risk to my survival?", "If that happened, would it really be so bad?", "Would I be the first person that had ever happened to?", "How many of my loved ones would stop loving me if that happened?".

This exercise will show your brain that you're taking its concerns into account and that, once you've analyzed them, only one or two – or none – of those fears are rooted in reality, so it needs to adjust its warning signals about them.

Strategy 3: Keep perspective

Sometimes, we get mad and feel "unfairly treated" by life when any setback occurs. "Why does everything happen to me?", "Can't anyone see how much I'm struggling with all these problems?", we ask ourselves.

The following technique involves putting your misfortune into perspective by comparing it with that of people around you. If necessary, remember that you are lucky compared to an enormous number of people who live every day with much worse problems: war, poverty, disease, violence...How many people in this world would gladly swap their problems for yours?

The perspective technique consists of ranking your emotions by comparing them with the ones you would be feeling now if you were going through those problems. For example, if you're really frustrated because you didn't get the delivery you were expecting or because a meeting got canceled last-minute (let's imagine you scored your frustration 7 on a scale from 0 to 10). If that's a 7, what intensity of frustration would you be feeling if you had no job to go to tomorrow? 500 out of 10? And if you were living in a refugee camp because your house got bombed? 1000 out of 10?

If you couldn't score your emotions any higher than 10, you would realize that your frustration about that canceled meeting would be 0.0001 compared to, for example, suffering from a degenerative disease.

I'm not trying to invalidate your thoughts or feelings. Sometimes, one little setback is enough to throw us off. What I want is for you not to overreact to something that's not that serious for you, because, AND THIS IS THE IMPORTANT PART: you are much stronger than you think. Don't let certain things bully you around; you've already shown so many times that you can cope with challenges.

This exercise will show you how your emotions begin to adapt to the real seriousness of the problem and leave room for feelings of gratitude for what you do have in life. This will give you greater strength to tackle the problems that really are hurting you.

Strategy 4: Speak well

Your thinking is informed by the way you communicate. Your words, whether directed at yourself or at others, influence your mood. In any conversation, your words will also affect the way people respond to you, which can generate emotions in return.

Do you speak nicely to yourself? Do you speak to others with respect, do you give constructive criticism, do you often yell, do you put yourself or others down, are you actively supportive, do you lie or manipulate? What is your speech and language like? I suggest that you analyze the following:

- Insults.

- Raised voice, yelling.

- Sarcasm, cynicism.

- Teasing (even if you're "just kidding").

- Lies.

- Discriminatory language based on race, sex, social status, etc.

- Pejorative language regarding physical appearance or disabilities.

- Pejorative language caused by envy.

- Violent, aggressive, challenging, intimidating language.

I invite you to write down in your diary all of the disrespectful expressions you detect, whether you say them out loud or to yourself. Next, write a reflection that questions or invalidates that negative expression. For example:

- *This guy is an idiot.* → I don't understand why that man is doing that. I can't figure out his reasoning and that makes me nervous.

- *I'm an idiot.* → I made a new mistake. I'll figure out whether it's due to tiredness, because I had incorrect information or because someone hindered me accidentally or on purpose.

- *Check her out, all well-dressed and made up. Sure, I mean she doesn't work...* → I feel envious of other people and that hinders me even more than the fact I don't have what they do. But my circumstances are different and I shouldn't be bitter about what others have.

- *You can't trust foreigners.* → You can't trust a lot of people, whether foreign or native. Labeling people when I don't know their reality or the reasons for their actions makes no sense. We should report and prosecute crime, but not cultural differences.

- *You don't want to see me if you don't do this.* → I'm using intimidation and covert threats, and that's violence. I urgently need to find another way to communicate.

The next step is to try to introduce those reflections into your mental discourse every time you find yourself getting mad. It may be difficult at first, but the more you practice, the more your mindset will change and you will feel much less tormented by your own emotions.

Strategy 5: Filter criticism

It's true that many people criticize with the intention of hurting, invalidating or sabotaging. But we often receive criticism that is right. That's why it's important to learn how to handle it. The first thing you need to do is accept that there's always going to be someone who criticizes you, no matter what you do. In fact, the more criticism you receive, the greater the evidence that you're moving forward.

So I advise you to listen to criticism and detect the kind that's genuine: usually, it comes from people who know the subject will and who don't see you as a threat. They tend to give the most sincere and useful criticism.

Note down all the criticism you receive in your daily life. Reflect on it, on how it makes you feel when it's said and on how you feel later, once you've analyzed it. In time, that immediate emotion and the emotion you feel once you have reflected on criticism will get closer to each other and eventually, criticism will only provoke one of two possible emotions: indifference, if it's trying to destabilize you, and gratitude if the criticism is correct and helps you to grow.

Cognitive defusion

Cognitive defusion is a method for changing your relationship with the thoughts and beliefs that bring you discomfort. Its name comes from "fusion" and it involves taking each of those thoughts and distancing yourself from them until they can't overcome you emotionally (stopping being fused to them – "de-fusing" yourself from them).

Cognitive defusion allows you to see uncomfortable or painful thoughts as unloaded mental events. To do this, use the following strategies:

- Repetition and deceleration: This consists of summing up the problematic thought in one sentence and repeating it increasingly slowly until it sounds hollow, like simple, meaningless sounds. For example: "A man assaulted me when I was sixteen", "My mother never wanted me", "I lose five years of my life to drinking", or "My partner left me for someone else and I think that person is better than me".

- Labeling thoughts: This involves mentally labeling the disturbing thoughts. For example: "Recurrent thought 1", "Unanalyzed thought", "New thought", "Speculation", "Opinion", "Possibility", and so on

- Chanting: Integrate the disturbing thoughts like familiar, calm song lyrics to diminish their emotional baggage.

- Observation of the thoughts like fleeting clouds that form and then disappear.

- Repetition of problematic thoughts out loud using an exaggerated or ridiculous tone of voice so you lose your fear of them and reduce their emotional impact.

- Relating the thought to an object and keeping that object in a box (real or imagined) so that only you can let it out when you want to. When it's time, throw that thought-object into the trash or the sea.

- Adopting the gratitude strategy: Give thanks to your brain for every thought it has, because you know it's only trying to help you understand it.

- Writing the thoughts down on paper and observing them from different points of view, like with physical distance until they become hard to read, in other languages, inserting random nonsense words into them and so on.

The aim of all of this is not to downplay your thoughts or traumatic memories, but to disarm them so they can't hold you back.

Practicing mindfulness

This method is the definitive tool for many people in terms of managing their emotions. Let's take another look at what it involves:

Mindfulness is a kind of mental training that acts on the emotions-thoughts-actions triangle. By practicing it regularly, you can live in awareness and consonance with yourself, as well as getting your pain and stress under control. How does it do that? By controlling the period of time between a stimulus and your response. Viktor Frankl[13] described it as follows:

---

[13] Viktor Frankl was a well-known Austrian neurologist and psychiatrist who survived three years' imprisonment in Nazi concentration camps. He wrote a book on his experiences: *Man's Search for Meaning*.

"Between stimulus and response there is a space. In that space is our power to choose our response. In our response lies our growth and our freedom."

Well, if we are so eaten up by anger that that space ceases to exist, or we react impulsively or act out of fear or prejudice, we are not free. Mindfulness works on making that space a true space for freedom of decision. How? Above all, through meditation: this trains the mind to focus on the present, accept it without reacting viscerally, and take what comes.

This is not a book on mindfulness (I do have one specifically on this topic, within this same collection [14]), but it's worth mentioning mindfulness, since it's proof that we can "talk" to our nervous system and guide our thoughts, emotions and actions to prevent them from overcoming us. If you still haven't tried this

---

[14] The Power of Mindfulness: *www.danieljmartin.es/books/pm*

ancient technique (it's been used for over 2,500 years), I invite you to give it a go!

Summary of Chapter 5

–   If you inform the way you think, you'll change the way you feel.

–   There are many strategies for restructuring pointless, stressful or invalidating thoughts. The aim of these strategies is to free us from the burden of having to "tend to" a series of thoughts that contribute nothing and are not adaptative.

–   Cognitive defusion is a method that seeks to change our relationship with thoughts and beliefs that cause discomfort, enabling us to distance ourselves from them and view them as mental events with no emotional baggage.

–   Mindfulness is a method of mental training that seeks to rebalance the way we react to our own thoughts.

Dominate your gale-force thoughts

"The emotion that can destroy you is always the emotion you ignore."

— Jim Rohn

Have you ever felt burning jealousy? Rage? Anxiety that made your chest tight? Hurricane-force emotions not only throw us to the ground, they often lead us to do things we later regret. And in the same way that we must redirect non-adaptative emotions, we need to do the same with those that appear like bolts from the blue.

"When I say manage emotions, I only mean the really distressing, incapacitating emotions. Feeling emotions is what makes life rich."

— Daniel Goleman

The 4 Horsemen of the Emotional Apocalypse: Anger, Envy, Jealousy and Guilt

Anger, envy, jealousy and guilt are four emotions that tend to get out of hand. As we've said, they are not dangerous in themselves (remember, emotions are neither good nor bad), but they do endanger us when we act in certain ways because of them. Me feeling envious of my sister because she's doing better than me is not dangerous. That envy leading me to hold distorted beliefs and act against my sister *is*.

It's one thing to accept that, at times, you can't avoid feeling envy. It's another thing to act inappropriately to "stop yourself from feeling it".

How to overcome envy

Of all the emotions I've studied, I think envy is the most treacherous.

Envy is the powerlessness of not possessing something we want and which other people do have. We tend to suffer it in silence because it makes us vulnerable; behind the envy, there is damaged self-esteem and a childish view of fairness. When we are under the effects of envy, we think: "it's not fair that that stupid guy earns more than me!".

The problem with envy (apart from the fact that it gives you a hard time) is that it leaves your satisfaction in the hands of what happens to other people: you get frustrated if your annoying neighbor is doing well, and you're glad when it goes wrong for him. You start to rely on what happens to him, and that means you're giving up control of your own wellbeing.

But you can tame envy. It might never fully disappear, but you can make it less aggressive. How? By analyzing it:

- What's bothering you so much? Is it your lack of the object itself, or is it feeling that the other person doesn't deserve it as much as you?

- Why does the other person not deserve it but you do?

- And why, if you deserve it more, don't you have it? What does it depend on?

- Is there something you can do to obtain it?

If the answer to the last question is "yes", you need to get to work. If the answer is "no", treat your frustration as if it were grief. You have to accept that, even if you do deserve it, the world doesn't always work that way. If that's the case, it tends to offer you something similar, as a substitute for the thing you can't get.

When you start to work on envy, it disappears. It's like magic; try it and you'll see.

Jealousy: a headless beast

Although the two are often confused, jealousy and envy are not the same thing. Envy is the desire for something you don't have, and jealousy is the fear of losing something you do have (like someone's love).

Kids get jealous when they see their moms cuddling their little brother or sister, dogs get jealous when their owners play with other animals, and most people get jealous when their partners get "too close" to someone else. Jealousy is the fear that the other person will discover there is *someone better* to give their love to and that they will abandon us.

Jealousy speaks to the way you experience love and your emotional bonds. In order to overcome it, you have to:

- Understand that you can't force anyone to love you: love is given voluntarily and freely.

- Work on your dependence: what would happen if you lost that person's love one day? What does that say about you? If that really panics you, does that mean you've placed your ability to be happy in someone else's hands?

- Work on the underlying reasons for the jealousy: is it because you feel inferior and are terrified of people finding out? Is it because, deep down, you don't believe you deserve love? Is it because you're harboring bitterness and can't trust anyone?

- Accept that your partner could leave you for someone else. That's just how it is. It's painful and scary, but nobody can be your property. You are also free to leave them. That doesn't excuse a lack of commitment, cheating or selfishness. I'm just saying nobody belongs to you.

- View jealousy as a ridiculous force; if someone is with you, it's because they want to be. You don't need to control them, pressure them or make a scene. As long as that person wants to be with you, it makes no sense to be jealous and it shows a lack of respect for your relationship. If that person decides to cheat on you or leave, there's no point feeling jealous; it won't change the situation.

Jealous is completely pointless. If you suspect or feel that that person is cheating on you or looking for someone else, you simply need to assess what's best for you. There are plenty more fish in the sea.

The poison of guilt

Guilt is the discomfort you feel when you know you have done something wrong when you could've done it right. And nobody can be at peace with themselves if they're eaten up by guilt.

Guilt is also a powerful weapon of manipulation when certain people discover it. In toxic relationships and dysfunctional families, it's common for one of the parties to use another's guilt for their own benefit. It's even possible for them to induce that guilt themselves. That's when guilt becomes a ticket to emotional blackmail.

In both cases, whether the guilt is personal or induced and provoked, it's contrary to your emotional wellbeing and you can't move forward until you overcome it. How can you do this?

There is a five-step process for this:

1. Admit responsibility with no ifs or buts: yes, you were in the wrong and you feel badly about it.

2. Understand why you did it: not in order to justify it, but to what you were hoping to achieve with that action.

3. Say sorry to the people you hurt, sincerely and without hoping for anything in return. It's no use saying: "I'm sorry, but that's just how I

am" or "Forgive me, although this wouldn't have happened if you hadn't...".

4. Take every possible course of action to try to repair the damage done.

5. Promise not to do it again, and keep that promise.

Sometimes, even after doing all that, we still feel guilty, or people forgive us but we still feel bad. Even so, if you do everything you can to repair the damage, your guilt should lessen. If not, you need to think about who has an interest in you continuing to harbor that guilt.

Sometimes, we carry guilt that was induced, unaware that it wasn't us who did wrong or that someone is using a mistake we made in order to exploit us. In these cases, you need to figure out where your responsibility ends. In order to determine the limit of your responsibility, the education you receive plays a fundamental role, not just at home but at school and in society – if you were educated in guilt, you are more likely to live in guilt without realizing it.

Many experts point to the church as an unstoppable guilt-generating machine. I agree with them: when a religion makes you feel guilty pretty much for just existing, that religion is violating your emotional rights and it's fair enough to leave it behind[15].

The same thing happens with anyone who takes advantage of your flaws (real or invented) in order to manipulate you, whether it's your boss, your mother or your partner. Don't let anyone exploit your feelings of guilt to benefit themselves.

Anger and the gray rock

---

[15] I'm not attacking anyone's faith here – I'm saying that no religion should use guilt as a weapon for control or subjugation.

I want to dedicate this section to a technique designed for dealing with people who drive you crazy. We all know a toxic or manipulative person, an undercover narcissist, someone who enjoys watching other people blow up. If you have someone like this near you and you can't get them out of your life, I advise you to use the gray rock method. The motto of this technique is RESPOND, DON'T REACT. It's about not giving these people the attention of the fight that they're after.

When a toxic person tries to provoke you, don't play their game. Turn your emotional volume down when you reply and be a boring gray rock: use neutral, impersonal phrases, be ambiguous in the face of their provocation, answer with humorless expressions (maybe, uh-huh, I guess, I don't really know) and so on. If the other person becomes more aggressive, respond to them unchangingly: "I'm sorry you're saying this", "I can't avoid you feeling that way", "What do you mean I'll regret this?", "I can see you're insulting me, are you okay?" and so on.

At first, you'll feel fake, and the other person will notice that, too. But if you keep going, you'll win: you'll be the gray rock that troublemakers and argumentative people keep banging up against:

"Emotional education is the ability to listen to almost anything without losing your temper or your self-confidence."

— Robert Frost

Discipline against anxiety

Although anxiety is a topic broad enough for entire books to itself, it's important to make some room for it here to highlight it as one of the hurricanes that tend to knock us down, lead us to act in ways we don't want to or, if we can manage to overcome it, leave us totally exhausted.

Remember that anxiety is a defense mechanism: it's your lizard brain sending you warning signals. The problem is that it sends you signals even when there is no real danger to your survival. So why does it do it?

When you have uncontrolled anxiety, you have a hypervigilant nervous system in the face of events that your brain links to your past, when you really were physically or psychologically compromised.

It would be silly to ignore anxiety or push it down with medication without having some therapy; repressed anxiety keeps coming back stronger until it's dealt with. What strategies can you use for dealing with anxiety?

1. **Talk to it**: Listen to it, feel all the emotions it brings you and ask it nicely to leave: "I'm sorry, but I can't see you right now", "I understand why you're here but I don't need

you", "I know what you're trying to tell me, but we're safe".

2. **Use relaxation techniques**: There are many resources, from meditation to therapeutic writing. If you do a relaxing activity during an anxiety spike, it will pass more quickly: remember, anxiety is fleeting.

3. **Show it who's boss**: Anxiety is your own insecurity telling you you can't do something. Find ways to get little wins so you grow in confidence and you can tell it that actually, you can.

4. **Confront anxiety with proof**: If your anxiety comes "dressed up" as a heart attack or "crazy" episode, you need to go to the doctor and get a diagnostic report to show that they are just anxiety attacks.

Summary of Chapter 6

– Some emotions, like anger, guilt, jealousy and envy, are more liable to derail you and lead you into dangerous behaviors.

– Envy is frustration at not having something others do, and it's a call to action – not toward others, but toward yourself.

– Jealousy is the fear of losing someone's love, and it's a jail cell you build around yourself.

– Guilt is self-reproach over an action that went against your values. Repairing the damage is the way to relieve it.

– Anxiety must be tended to before it can disappear.

The triangle of integrity

"Every emotion has its place, but it shouldn't interfere with the right thing to do."

— Susan Oakey-Baker

So far, we've looked at what emotions are, how they work, how they relate to your thoughts and behaviors, and how you can regulate them. Now, we're going to look at how your actions feed into your emotions and how you can manage them through what you do. To do this, we need to talk about personal integrity.

What is personal integrity?

We say that a person has integrity when they don't sell out or allow themselves to be corrupted. In psychology, personal integrity happens when your actions correspond to your values and convictions. In other words, when you are loyal to yourself and your actions are a consequence of what you believe and feel.

While the triangle of the nervous system united the concepts of thoughts, emotions and actions, the triangle of integrity unites your value system, your feelings and your actions in relation to them.

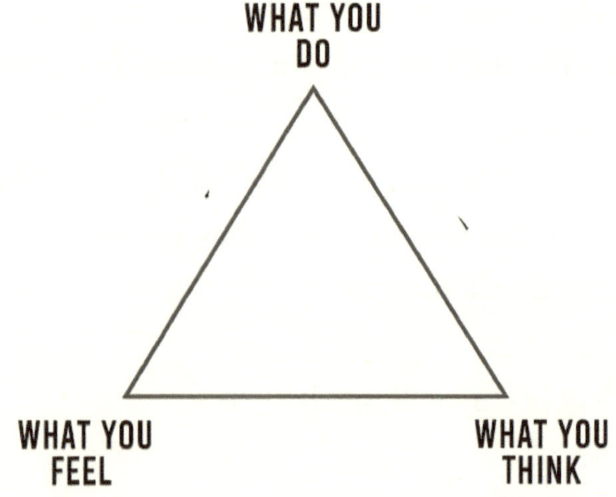

What does this have to do with emotional management? Well, as soon as you stop acting in accordance with that triangle, emotional discomfort begins.

Practicing integrity

If you want to live in peace, you must practice integrity. That means that, if you're a person committed to your job, you must act accordingly: take your tasks seriously, be honest and find satisfaction in doing your duty. When you don't do that (if you cheat or mistreat your coworkers), you'll feel like a sellout.

This happens because, when you behave in a way that matches your value system, you feel good. If you betray yourself, you begin to feel uncomfortable inside: your own conscience is telling you something doesn't add up.

You can't have emotional wellbeing if you don't feel like you're doing the right thing in terms of who you are or want to be: your happiness relies on your dignity and your personal integrity. Of course, there are things that make us happy that have nothing to do with personal ethics (eating ice cream, for example). And it's not that those things are bad or unimportant, it's just that they're not essential for fulfilment. Why? Because no ice cream (or sports car, or luxury cruise) will make you feel good if your triangle of integrity is broken.

It's true that practicing integrity doesn't guarantee happiness, but not doing so does guarantee eternal unhappiness. So what do you do in order to have integrity? How do you manage the triangle of integrity in your daily life so that you don't feel bad emotionally? Follow these steps:

1. **Know your own values:** What do you think is important to defend in life? Where do you draw the line ethically? Could you write it down in your journal? For example: would

you have any ethical conflict if you stole from a vulnerable person? What if you robbed a millionaire? Would you speak up for someone who needed it if doing so hurt you in some way? Under what circumstances would you gladly break the law?

2. **Find the relation between these and your current lifestyle:** In your family, with your partner, at work, as a citizen, as a member of a community...Are you acting in accordance with your principles? Is there any activity in your life that goes against your own moral conscience?

3. **Be honest with yourself and with others**: Try to lead an honest life. It's true that society often forces us to lie, but nobody can force us to lie to ourselves. The less we do so, the more we can control our emotional wellbeing.

4. **Fulfil your responsibilities:** Stick to the commitments and promises you make. Few

things are more gratifying in life than giving your word and keeping it.

5. **Foster your own and others' authenticity**: Don't try to be someone you're not, and don't try to force others to change.

6. **Be willing to improve and grow**: Life offers constant motivation to be curious and keep learning. Never think you know it all or that you don't need to discover anything new.

Every action carries an emotion

The greatest doses of emotional wellbeing come from the good results of your actions in line with your values. To reach this, you need to have life goals and purposes that inspire you.

What are life purposes?

Life purposes (or meanings, or deep motivations) are the ultimate reasons you're living for. They are the voluntary personal missions you set yourself and that help you to know who you are and what you want your place in the world to be.

We all have something we really want. Something we like doing or that we could dedicate days or years to. When we get the chance, we make that our life's work by turning it into our career or our world. If we're less lucky, we make it something to keep us company in our spare time.

Do you know what you're good at, or what you most want? Is it close to becoming a life purpose for you? It doesn't need to be significant for all mankind; you just need to be able to relate to it and for it to make sense to you.

Here are some of the life purposes my clients have told me about:

- Being a good pediatrician.

- Being the best possible husband.

- Forming a family where everyone is loved and happy.

- Contribute to improving my town.

- Fighting poverty.

- Creating a successful app.

- Starting a band.

- Organizing a cultural event that keeps going for years.

- Making my kids proud of me.

If you're not clear on your life purposes, you can work backwards: don't think about what you want to achieve, think about what you want to avoid. What are your purpose in reverse – what point do you never want to get to?

And bear in mind that loving doing something is reason enough to do it, regardless of its outcome.

Acceptance and Commitment Therapy

Acceptance and commitment therapy (ACT) is used particularly to accept traumatic past experiences or difficult current situations. It was developed by American clinical psychologist Steven C. Hayes in the eighties and it's based on redirecting the person toward their own values and personality, not toward what happened or is happening to them.

ACT encourages people to be fully aware of their thoughts, emotions and behaviors without fighting them. Once you're aware of them, this therapy seeks to make patients commit to acting in accordance with their values, objectives and way of being, rather than according to those stressful experiences or circumstances. In other words: keep going despite the situation.

To achieve this, it fosters the learning of attention skills and the adoption of a broader perspective on life itself. This therapy uses techniques such as cognitive defusion in order to reduce the impact of certain experiences.

Transversal habits for practicing integrity

Finally, let's take a look at some additional strategies for "bulking up" your triangle of integrity:

- **Surround yourself with emotionally healthy people.** We know that nobody's perfect, but the environment you move in affects you a lot. If you're surrounded by toxic people, distance yourself. If you can't right now, try not to absorb it or get emotionally involved.

- **Persevere.** Don't quit your projects at the first hurdle. Don't be a conformist who can't grow. Commit to acting each and every day.

- **Embrace a sense of humor.** If it were a food, humor would be a powerhouse of antioxidants: laughter can pick you up and improve your outlook on the world.

- **Know yourself.** Knowing yourself, your strengths and your areas for improvement is fundamental for emotional resilience. Reflect on your values, beliefs and goals in life.

- **Develop a growth mindset.** Adopt an attitude of constant learning and take challenges as opportunities to outdo yourself.

- **Set realistic goals.** Have achievable aims that work with you. Divide your goals into smaller steps and celebrate any progress.

- **Look for positive perspectives.** Focus on the positives and seek to learn even in difficult situations. Cultivate gratitude and practice realistic optimism.

- **Sleep well.** Sleep is a basic need as well as an emotional one. Prioritize this if you don't already have good sleep habits.

- **Smile more.** We already know that spontaneous smiles are more genuine than forced ones, but even forced smiles help, since your brain will release endorphins either way.

Summary of Chapter 7

–   Just like your thoughts and beliefs, your actions affect your thoughts, too.

–   To balance out the triangle between what you think, what you feel and what you do, you must practice integrity.

–   Integrity means living according to your own values and it's the principal source of emotional wellbeing.

–   Working on the journey and living with purpose strengthens the triangle of integrity.

Be emotional, be happy!

You've reached the end of the book! How did it go? How do you feel? I hope you've felt good about it and that you've found lots of useful material in these pages.

For my part, all that's left is to congratulate you for taking your own emotions seriously. Not many people do, and believe me, there is no happiness without a stable emotional system. So WELL DONE.

Together with this, I want to tell you that I hope you go far in this process of knowing, understanding and guiding your own emotions. I believe I've shown you a good 7-step method to help you along the way. You might have found some sections more useful than others, or you might have found some things quite shocking and revealing. But I hope that all together, it helps you.

Because if you've come this far, it's because you want to grow and improve. And I know you can do it – wanting to is half the work. But you do need to work. Don't let your daily routine eat away at your priorities. Don't let your emotions return to their same old corner, where they only come out when you can't take any more. Bring them to the foreground. Let them show! Remember that they're your allies.

Lots of people talk about emotional management, but not many people practice it. You're on track already. The fact you read this book means you're one step ahead of people who just settle for good intentions.

Listen to yourself. Remember all the reasons you have for doing so. Don't refuse to feel, don't settle for less. Don't stop "being intense". That's what life is about! Life is made to be felt deeply, passionately and constantly – not to be feared.

Be emotional and be happy!

Daniel

Your opinion is very important

As I'm an independent author, your opinion is so important to me and to future readers like you. I would be hugely grateful if you would leave me **a review on your favorite store** to tell me what you thought of my book **so that I can keep on improving it**:

- What did you like best?
- Is there anything you felt was missing
- Who would you recommend it to?
- ...

A gift just for you!

Would you like to **read my next book completely FREE?** Scan the code below and **join my readers' club!**

Great surprises await: be the first to read my new releases, listen to my audiobooks for free, get signed and dedicated copies... and much more!

www.danieljmartin.es/readersclub/

Other books by Daniel J. Martin

www.danieljmartin.es/wide/books